The Student Survival Guide

The Student Survival Guide

Second Edition

By
Phil Chambers
&
Elaine Colliar

ECPC Publications
(A division of Learning Technologies Ltd)

Learning Technologies Ltd

Elaine Colliar
TRAINING YOU REMEMBER

Published by:
ECPC Publications
A division of Learning Technologies Ltd
The Forge
New Invention
Bucknell
Shropshire SY7 0BS
United Kingdom

www.learning-tech.co.uk

First Edition 2004
Second Edition 2008

Mind Map® is a registered trademark of the Buzan Group used under licence

A catalogue record for this book is available from the British Library

ISBN 978-1-904906-03-2

Cover design by Yves Van Damme (Pangraphics Ltd)

Printed and bound by WPG Ltd, Welshpool, Powys, Wales

Dedication

This book is dedicated to every student who has ever thought that there must be an easier way to balance their studies, their hobbies and their lives. We hope that by showing them the path travelled by students before them, they can find an easier route.

To my baby boy, James Daniel, a learning laboratory in our daily life together. The boy who has spurred me on to braver and bigger things than I could ever have dreamed possible.

Finally, to Eddie Mara, a remarkable teacher who first introduced me to Mind Mapping and changed the course of my life forever.

Elaine Colliar

To the excellent teachers who helped me throughout my school days and to those who now attend my seminars, taking the techniques in this book into classrooms around the World.

Phil Chambers

ACKNOWLEDGEMENTS

Tony Buzan - For originating Mind Mapping
Neil & Stewart Denley - For marketing assistance
Rod Dumbreck - For technical help
Anne Jones - For proof reading and support
Sarah Jameson - For proof reading second edition
Vanda North - For training us both in the art of radiance

Contents List

Contents Mind Map

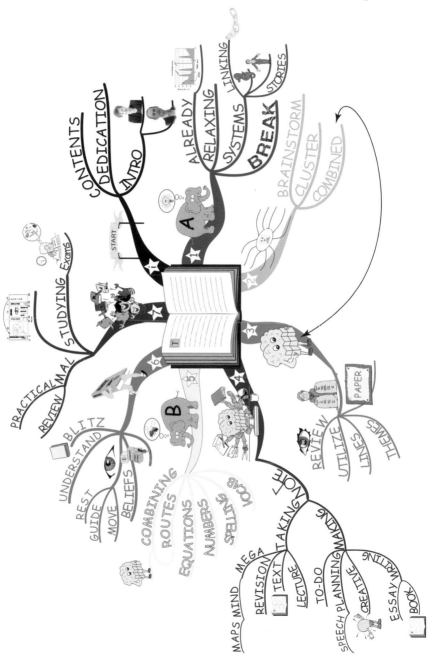

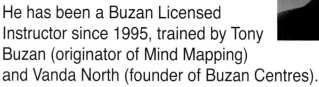

PHIL

Phil Chambers is the reigning World Mind Mapping Champion. He is a six times Mind Sports Olympiad Medalist and International Grandmaster of Mind Mapping.

He has been a Buzan Licensed Instructor since 1995, trained by Tony Buzan (originator of Mind Mapping) and Vanda North (founder of Buzan Centres).

In addition to this, he is a Registered Accelerated Learning Trainer, a Practitioner of Neuro-Linguistic Programming (NLP), an Associate of the Chartered Institute of Personnel & Development (CIPD) and a member of the Professional Speakers Association.

Prior to entering the training profession, Phil worked as a computer programmer and has a BSc in Physics and Chemistry from the University of Durham.

Phil is Chief Arbiter of the World Memory Sports Council and won the "Special Services to Memory" award in 1996.

His Mind Maps have been published in GCSE Revision Guides, "The Learning Revolution" and "Teaching Pupils How To Learn". He is co-author of "A Mind to do Business" and sole author of "101 Top Tips for Better Mind Maps".

You can contact Phil through his training company, Learning Technologies Ltd, details at the back of this book.

ELAINE

Elaine Colliar is the five times World Mind Mapping Champion and an International Grandmaster of Mind Mapping. She hosts seminars in Mind Mapping, Memory, Mental and Financial Literacy around the world.

As a dyslexic, trained by the Buzan Centre several years ago, Elaine specialises in introducing these techniques, not only to Multi-National Companies but to the educationally disenfranchised everywhere she is invited.

Starting her working life in London's West End as a stage manager and club manager, she is now classed as a serial entrepreneur. Elaine has founded a string of companies including: Btex - an award winning IT and website development company (the developers of streetmap.co.uk), Business Unusual - a highly successful corporate training company, Invest n Share - a stock market education and investment club network and, most recently, Building Success Ltd - a property investment company.

She is a highly accomplished trainer, qualified to teach all of the courses offered through the Buzan Centre, as well as several developed by herself. She was also involved in the production of Hodder & Stoughton's GCSE and A-Level Revision Guides and co-authored "A Mind to do Business."

Despite great success as a business woman, her proudest achievement is her seven-year-old son, James.

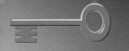

MEMORY PART A
INTRODUCTION

In this section we will explore what you already do to remember and forget and discover your brain's natural memory rhythms.

You will see how to:

Improve your memory with a simple link system and how this can be made stronger by using some general principles.

Use your body to help you remember!

Review informtation easily that has been memorised in a brain friendly way.

Boost recall by taking breaks.

To begin, give yourself 2 minutes to try to remember the following list of words...

book	the	and
of	and	stop
the	hand	own
white	walk	time
and	work	hold
of	William Shakespeare	of
end	candle	house
the	hill	coat

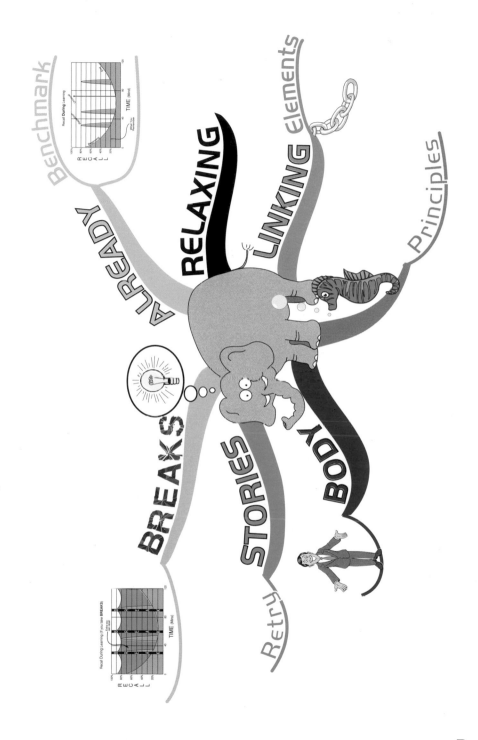

WHAT YOU ALREADY DO

Can you recall all the words in the correct order?

1 _____	9 _____	17_____
2 _____	10 _____	18_____
3 _____	11 _____	19_____
4 _____	12 _____	20_____
5 _____	13 _____	21_____
6 _____	14 _____	22_____
7 _____	15 _____	23_____
8 _____	16 _____	24_____

If you can't answer this test correctly, don't worry. The list is designed to be too long for you to remember on reading it through once unless you are using a memory system.

Psychologists have determined that, on average, you can hold 7±2 pieces of data in short-term memory at the same time.

Can you remember any of the first few words?

Can you remember the exact middle word?

Can you recall any of the last words?

Did any words jump out at you as being unusual?

Did any of the words you read have any strong associations for you – or did any of the words you read combine to make a single mental picture or thought?

Did you recognise if any of the words were repeated?

On average the recall pattern looks like this...

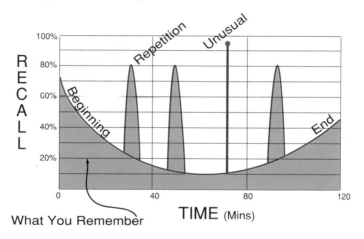

So to make things more memorable you need to:

⭐ **Have more beginnings and ends to your learning.**

⭐ **Repeat or link things together to create strong associations.**

⭐ **Make things unusual or outstanding.**

INTRODUCTION

WHAT YOU
ALREADY DO

**RELAXATION
AND MEMORY**

LINK SYSTEM

SEAHORSE
PRINCIPLES

BODY SYSTEM

YOUR REVIEW

BREAKS

SUMMARY

RELAXATION
AND MEMORY

Has your mind ever gone blank in the middle of an exam?

Have you ever had someone's name 'on the tip of your tongue'?

You knew that you knew it but couldn't quite remember it and the harder you tried to remember the more elusive the memory became. Then when you stopped trying and relaxed the information just popped into your head.

What physically happens when you are stressed is that your brain goes into 'fight or flight' mode - Faced with danger the best survival strategy inherited from our caveman ancestors was to fight or run away. Blood and oxygen are diverted from the upper part of your brain where memories are stored down to your muscles. So you're physically strengthened but mentally weakened.

The way to stop your mind from going blank is to avoid getting stressed. There are some simple relaxation techniques which, when practiced regularly, will allow you to enter a state of relaxed alertness that is ideal for learning whenever you need to.

Here's what you do:

- Find somewhere quiet and comfortable to sit, away from distractions.
- Close your eyes and breathe in through your nose and out through your mouth. With each out breath give a little sigh 'ahh' and count slowly backwards from ten to one. With each number feel the stress drain out of you.
- Imagine being somewhere tranquil where you can you feel relaxed and safe. Perhaps on a warm tropical beach, in a forest or in the mountains. Imagine the sights, smells, sounds, tastes and physical sensations as if you were really there.
- Spend as long as you like.
- When you're ready to return, count slowly back from one to ten, the scene fading with each number. When you reach ten, open your eyes and feel refreshed and relaxed.

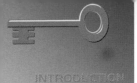

THE LINK MEMORY SYSTEM

The Link System is one of the simplest memory systems but is none the less quite powerful. It makes use, primarily, of the fact that you remember associated items.

To remember a list you take each item and associate it in some way with the next. This forms a chain of associations that can easily be recalled.

If the list contains abstract concepts these will need to be symbolised by concrete objects.

As an example, let's try to memorise the first 10 chemical elements in the Periodic Table:

Hydrogen	Carbon
Helium	Nitrogen
Lithium	Oxygen
Beryllium	Fluorine
Boron	Neon

These can be remembered as follows…

Imagine a huge tower-block sized, shiny red fire hydrant (HYDROGEN). As you walk past you look up and see millions of helium - filled (HELIUM) balloons tied to the top of the hydrant. There are so many that they begin to lift the hydrant up off the ground and into the air.

As it rises into the evening sky, you follow its route, as it is lit by the intense white light (LITHIUM) shining from thousands of berries (BERYLLIUM) on a nearby tree. At the base of the tree is an ugly wart-faced smelly wild boar (BORON) digging at the roots and throwing up a pile of dirty black coal (CARBON).

The dust and soot from the ever increasing pile of coal blocks out the Sun and causes a false night (NITROGEN). The airborne dust makes it so hard for you to breathe that you don a diving suit and oxygen tank (OXYGEN). You struggle to waddle forward wearing your flippers, this makes you sweat and breathe heavily.

You remove your mask and you realise that you are coming down with a case of the flu (FLUORINE). You begin to cough and splutter and as you sneeze you spray mucus over a massive neon (NEON) sign in the shape of a number 10 that blinks on and off in front of you.

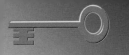

SEAHORSE PRINCIPLES

In simple terms, memories are pictures that you create in your head. The clearer and more detailed the picture, the easier it is to recall.

By using the following 8 easy principles to add to the pictures you create in your head you will be able to make unforgettable memories with ease:

Senses

Making a memory more "multi-sensory" by using as many of your senses as you can (ie sight, sound, smell, taste and touch) will make the memory trace much stronger and easier to recall.

Exaggeration

By creating pictures that are larger, louder, smellier, sweeter, sourer and mare tactile you can boost what you remember.

Action

Create your images with as much action as possible. A full-colour horse galloping through a field with rippling muscles, flowing mane and high pitched whinny is more memorable than a black and white image of a static horse.

Humour

Things that make you smile, giggle or groan – even bad jokes and puns will increase your enjoyment of learning and therefore increase your memory.

Order

Ordered items are easier to recall than those that are jumbled up. One of the first ways we learn is when our carers tell us stories where things must happen in a certain order.

Repetition

Repetition – especially at the appropriate times – boosts what you can remember. It reinforces the memory pathways in the brain making it easier and easier to remember what you are trying to learn every time you return and do a review of that information.

Symbols

Using symbols boosts recall – especially as memories are pictures. Substituting abstract or ordinary items with extraordinary symbols will make them easier to remember (more about how you use symbolism to translate information into an easier to remember form later…).

Enjoy

Using your memory and your imagination to learn should be easy and fun. If you can make it fun to do, you will want to keep doing it. A well trained imagination will help make memorising a delight.

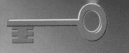

By combining the SEAHORSE principles with any of the memory or study systems you will greatly improve your ability to remember any information that you choose.

The hippocampus, a structure in the centre of the brain thought to be responsible for memory is so called because of its SEAHORSE-like shape.

THE BODY LIST SYSTEM

Have you ever written down a list of things you need to remember – and then discovered that you can't remember where you put the list?

Here is an easy technique that helps you create a useful short term memory system that will help you remember any things that you would normally put on a list - ie shopping lists, to-do lists, etc.

NOTE: If you don't use the other systems in this book then this is the technique you need for cramming if all else fails!

The body has a number of parts in set locations that can act as places (or hooks) to 'hang' objects in your imagination:

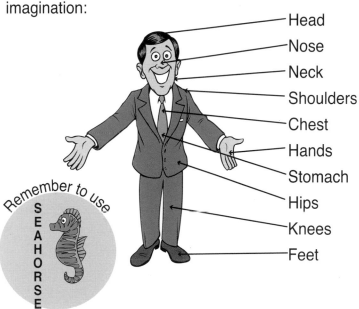

Head
Nose
Neck
Shoulders
Chest
Hands
Stomach
Hips
Knees
Feet

Remember to use
S
E
A
H
O
R
S
E

For example, to remember the first three items of a shopping list...

ON YOUR FEET:
Imagine you are balanced on a pile of eggs. You are too heavy for them and they smash, 'squishing' yolk between your toes as you smell their rotten stench.

BETWEEN YOUR KNEES:
A loaf of French bread - Smell the aroma of a fresh 2m long loaf that makes you walk awkwardly to prevent from falling.

ON YOUR HIPS:
A bunch of bananas on each hip: Huge, dangling, fluorescent yellow.

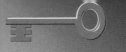

YOUR REVIEW

To show just how easy it is to memorise information using these techniques and to act as a review, try to fill in the blanks for the examples that we have used so far in this section…

What do the letters in **SEAHORSE** stand for?

S_____

E_____

A_____

H_____

O____

R_____

S_____

E____

What were the three shopping list items?

_____

_____

_____

Fill in the blanks in the Periodic Table story:

Imagine a huge tower-block sized, shiny red fire hydrant (_____). As you walk past you look up and see millions of _____ - filled (_____) balloons tied to the top of the hydrant. There are so many that they begin to lift the hydrant up off the ground and into the air.

As it rises into the evening sky, you follow its route, as it is lit by the intense white light (_____) shining from thousands of _____ (BERYLLIUM) on a nearby tree. At the base of the tree is an ugly wart-faced smelly wild boar (_____) digging at the roots and throwing up a pile of dirty black coal (_____).

The dust and soot from the ever increasing pile of coal blocks out the Sun and causes a false night (_____). The airborne dust makes it so hard for you to breathe that you don a diving suit and _____ tank (_____). You struggle to waddle forward wearing your flippers, this makes you sweat and breathe heavily.

You remove your mask and you realise that you are coming down with a case of the __ (FLUORINE). You begin to cough and splutter and as you sneeze you spray mucus over a massive _____ (_____) sign in the shape of a number 10 that blinks on and off in front of you.

BREAKS

MYTH

In order to learn something you have to hit the books for hours and hours until you have drilled it into your head.

TRUTH

The best way to learn is to approach it as 'little and often'. Work for a while, then when your brain starts to daydream, or wander, or drift away, or get bored, **STOP**, take a break and start learning again.

You can actually remember much more from a period of learning if you break it down into little chunks than if you do it all in one go...

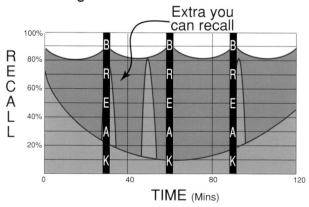

So you can recall more by working less. Don't work harder, **work smarter**!

SUMMARY

When studying:

⭐ **Have more beginnings and ends to your learning.**

⭐ **Repeat or link things together to create strong associations.**

⭐ **Make things unusual or outstanding.**

Practice relaxation techniques to avoid stress in exams.

The Link System can be used to remember simple lists.

The Seahorse Principles aid and reinforce memory systems:

Senses
Exaggeration
Action
Humour
Order
Repetition
Symbols
Enjoy

The Body List system can be used to remember 10 items or more.

Take regular breaks whilst studying to boost recall.

CHAPTER TWO

BRAINSTORMING
& CLUSTERING

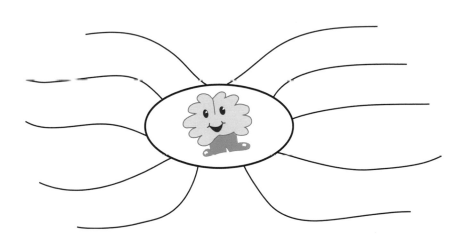

BRAINSTORMING

Brainstorming is a way to express and freely associate ideas as they come to you without the need to classify them. Write down everything that comes to mind without judging the ideas. A stupid idea can often lead to a good idea that you may not have otherwise thought of.

Begin by drawing a picture of the topic that you re thinking about in the centre of your sheet of paper with lines radiating outwards.

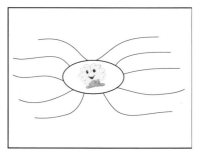

Write words or draw pictures of the ideas on these lines. If you run out of ideas add extra lines, as the brain likes to complete things and will generate enough ideas to fill the available spaces.

If you find that an idea that you have written triggers related ideas, these can be written on smaller lines off the main ones…

You can even add
lines to the lines…

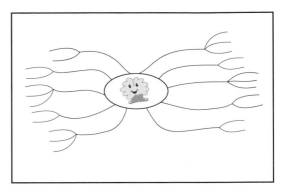

and so on….

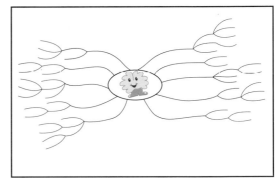

For ever …
and ever…
and ever…

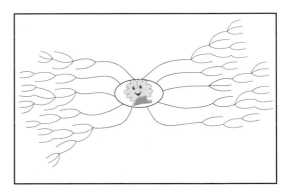

CLUSTERING

Once you have taken your thinking wide with a
brainstorm, it is often useful to improve the focus and
clarity of your ideas by grouping them together into
categories…

For example if your brainstorm
generated the following ideas…

These could be grouped into:

- Ingredients
- Occasions
- Feelings
- Places

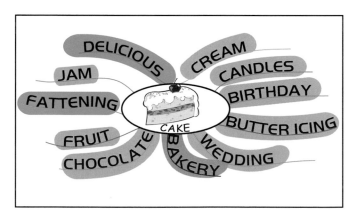

These categories can be used as the
main branches of a Mind Map - The
technique that we'll show you in the next
section of this book…

COMBINING THE TECHNIQUES

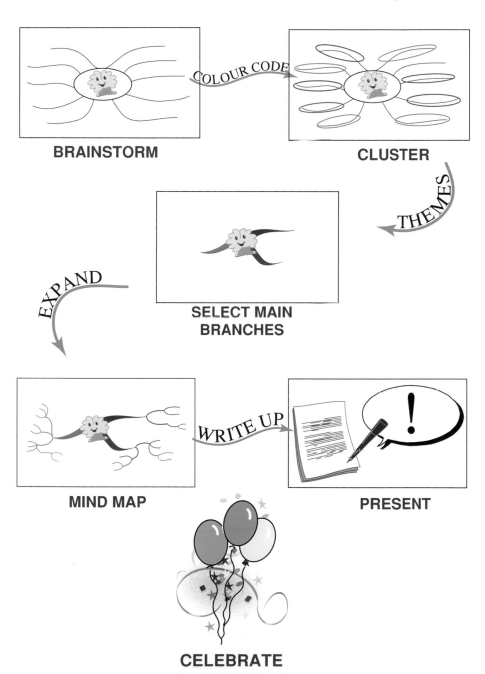

BRAINSTORM

COLOUR CODE

CLUSTER

THEMES

SELECT MAIN
BRANCHES

EXPAND

MIND MAP

WRITE UP

PRESENT

CELEBRATE

CHAPTER THREE

MIND MAPPING RULES

INTRODUCTION

What is Mind Mapping?

Mind Mapping is the most efficient note making and note taking technique that we know.

It works in harmony with the rhythms of the brain by using images, associations, space and colour to encourage thought processes to flow and increase recall.

A Mind Map is a powerful graphical representation of your thoughts and ideas - reflecting on paper the structure of your brain and how it processes information.

In this section you will learn the rules that you follow to create a Mind Map. These are all based on psychological research and many years of experience and so you should try to adhere to them wherever possible, especially if you're using a Mind Map for studying or to increase your memory.

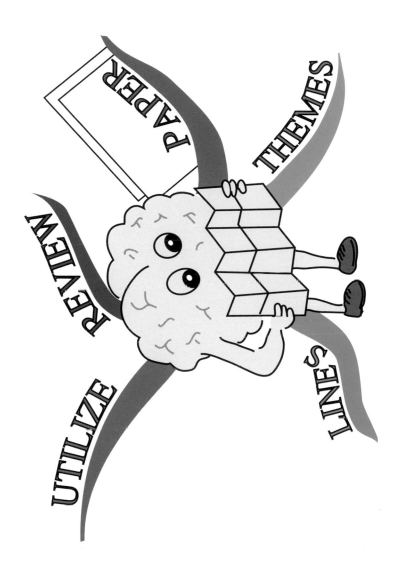

THE RULES OF MIND MAPPING

Central Image

Create a unique and therefore memorable central image for each Mind Map you make. If you feel your artwork lets you down, get creative and copy, cut and paste, photocopy or print out a central image from another source.

Take the time to make a beautiful starting point to your Mind Map - using at least 3 colours will boost your recall by making the unique image more memorable, but use as many colours as you can.

By taking the time and effort to make a central image you are preparing the brain to look forward to a learning experience.

PAPER

Use your paper landscape (long side along the top) - because our writing tends to be longer than higher, this leaves you more room for branching out with your associations.

Use blank paper - if you use lined or squared paper you may find you use the straight lines for writing on rather than flowing outwards in a radiant way.

Use as large a piece of paper as you can - A3 paper will leave you plenty of space to capture lots of detail on your Mind Map. For ease of filing and to be able to carry the Mind Maps around school or college, why not fold and file them like this...

File by subject

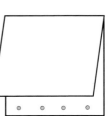

Punch

Fold with a margin

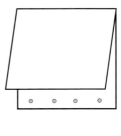

A3 paper

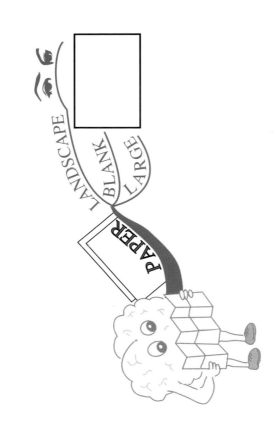

LANDSCAPE

BLANK

LARGE

PAPER

central image with the less important details out towards the edges. The order flows from the 2 o'clock position clockwise.

WORDS

Mind Maps only use key words. They tend to be nouns and will usually comprise 5 – 10% of the words. This means that you will be capturing far fewer words taking notes on a Mind Map than if you were taking "traditional" linear notes. Printing words (in upper or lower case) helps the brain to "photograph" the words more easily to recall at a later date. Using one word per line allows you to make more associations from each word and so improve your memory.

THEMES - IMAGES

Start by creating a unique image in the centre of your paper. After reviewing you will discover that you can recreate the Mind Map in your mind's eye. A unique image will help you to do this. Use at least three colours to make the image more attractive and hence memorable. Don't draw a box around your central image. Leaving the image open with no boundaries drawn around it helps you to associate more freely and widely.

HIERARCHY

A Mind Map has a radiant hierarchy. The most important facts are clustered in close to the

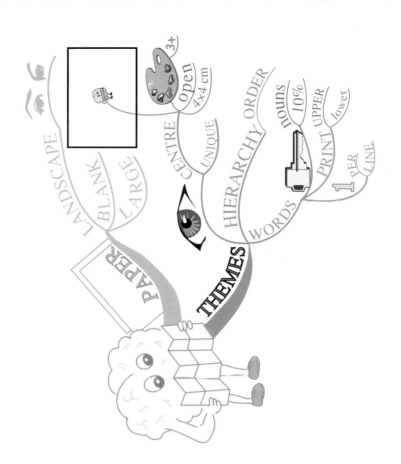

Try to use no more than 7 main branches on each Mind Map (short term memory can hold 7±2 bits of information at a time) -fewer branches often lead to enhanced memory.

Using organic or wavy main branches in a Mind Map helps to draw the eye outwards. By using curved lines you are also best able to use the space on the paper, by curving the lines into the space available.

Using one colour for each branch provides an extra memory hook to increase the ease with which you can recall your information - "It's on the green branch" … "It's a long word, etc."

LINES

Make the length of each line equal to the length of the keyword or image on it. Too short and it won't fit, too long and you waste space! Make sure that each line connects to the end of the previous line and that the lines radiate out from the centre. Often if you leave a gap between lines you will fail to recall things 'downstream' of the break.

The lines should decrease in size and hence importance towards the outside of the Mind Map. At the centre they are thick like the branches of a tree, becoming thinner and thinner before tapering off into tiny twigs.

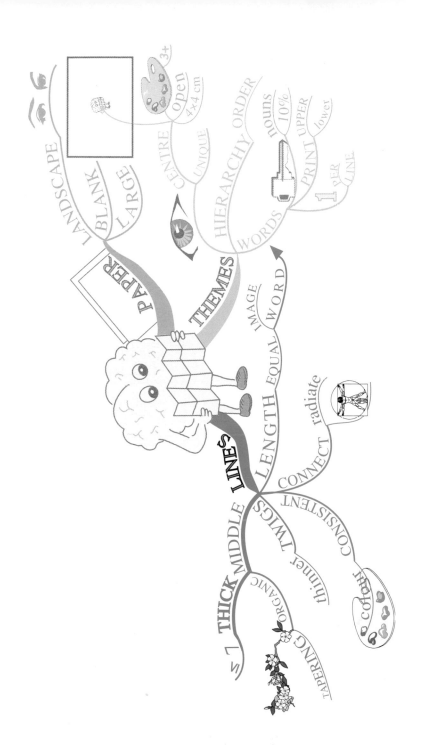

Make each new Mind Map just a little bit more beautiful to your own senses. Use lettering that you enjoy looking at, your favourite colours and images.

Have fun creating your Mind Map – if something is fun to do then you want to do more of it. So include humour, jokes, cartoons, puns (especially terrible ones)!

A Briefcase!

UTILIZE

Mind Mapping is a fun and creative way of making and taking notes. To keep the fun, keep your brain engaged and to help boost your recall, try to improve each Mind Map by increasing the use of each of these concepts every time.

If information is very important or relevant, you can use perspective to make the image look 3-dimensional rather than making it look flat – the information will then jump off the Mind Map and into your memory.

The difference between an 'A' grade and an 'A plus' is the ability to show how knowledge from one subject connects to another.

You should not be surprised if the same word crops up on more than one branch of your Mind Map. This shows that the repeated word is a new theme running through the topic that you may not have seen had you been using linear notes. When you notice a word appearing on multiple branches you can reinforce the connection and hence your memory of the information by linking each occurrence with arrows.

Leonardo da Vinci said, "Study the Art of Science and the Science of Art. Develop the senses and realise that everything is connected to everything else".

We are programmed to enjoy colour. All around us in the natural world there is vibrant colour. Rather than create boring, monotonous, monotone notes in black pen on white paper, rejoice in using multi-coloured pens, pencils, paints etc on the best quality paper you can find. Have fun experimenting with the hundreds of makes of pens on the market; fat pens; thin nibs; gel colours, glitter pens and scented pens. Use as many different types as you can to boost what you can remember.

ARROWS

One of the best ways to increase your understanding of the world – and to improve your exam grades at the same time is to become aware of how information is connected together.

As well as being used as a shorthand for particular concepts, codes can be used to indicate connections between related ideas. For example, if the same word occurs several times in a Mind Map you could either link each occurrence with an arrow or simply put the same code symbol (such as a star) next to each occurrence.

You can also colour code your Mind Map. For example on a 'things to do' Mind Map you can use highlighter pens to code urgent tasks in pink, things that rely on other people in blue and completed things in yellow. Similarly, on a revision Mind Map, important or related concepts can be colour coded in the same way.

SENSES

Have you ever smelt a certain scent like the smell of fresh bread or a particular brand of perfume and been vividly reminded of a distant memory? It's not just smells that evoke powerful memories. Every experience is a combination of inputs from all your senses. So try to use words and images on your Mind Maps that evoke as many of your other senses as possible.

CODES

Letters and words are just codes that symbolise ideas. Likewise, road signs, icons on your computer, musical notes and numbers are also codes. Try to build up a library of your own code symbols that represent concepts that occur regularly on your Mind Maps.

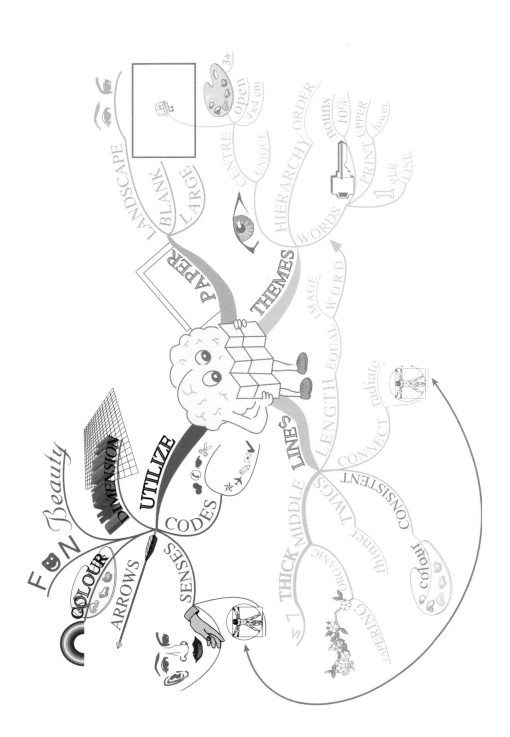

Simply strike through the appropriate code after you have completed each review.

The beauty of reviewing using a Mind Map is that it can take so little time to do. A complex Mind Map containing a whole afternoon's learning can be reviewed in as little as 90 seconds. The entire review process takes less than 10 minutes to give you almost perfect recall of the information you have captured.

REVIEW

Be like the elephant – decide that you are never going to forget. By reviewing your Mind Maps at the appropriate times i.e. 10 minutes after creating, then 1 day, 1 week, 1 month and 3 months later you maximise your chances of remembering everything you have noted down.

To help you keep track of when you need to review, date the Mind Map at the bottom and enter the review codes:

10, D, W, M, 3M

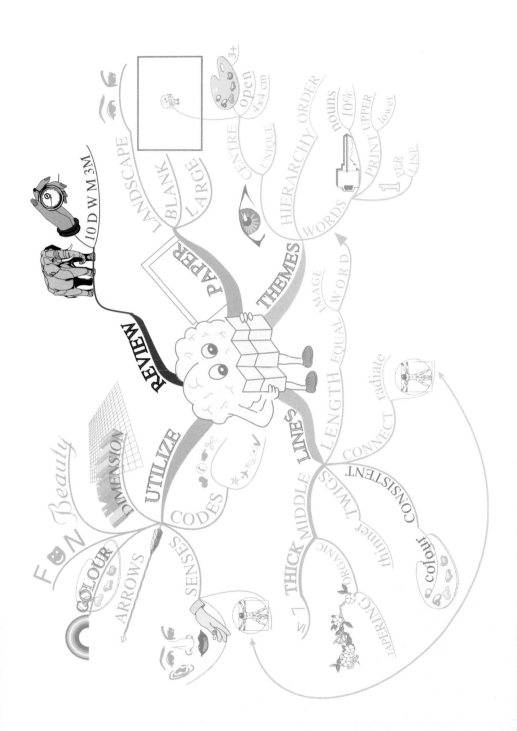

SUMMARY

CHAPTER FOUR

APPLICATIONS OF MIND MAPPING

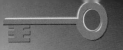

INTRODUCTION

Having learned how to Mind Map, we will now explore some of the many applications of Mind Maps in studying and everyday life.

Our list is neither meant to be prescriptive nor exhaustive. Once you begin to build confidence and become comfortable with the technique, you will discover many more applications for Mind Maps.

The applications can broadly be divided into two categories:

Note Making - expressing your own ideas on paper:

WRITING A BOOK
AN ESSAY PLAN
A CREATIVE MIND MAP
PLANNING A SPEECH
TO-DO LIST

Note Taking - taking someone else s ideas and understanding or remembering them:

LECTURE NOTES
NOTES FROM A TEXT BOOK
CURRICULUM REVISION
MEGA MIND MAPS

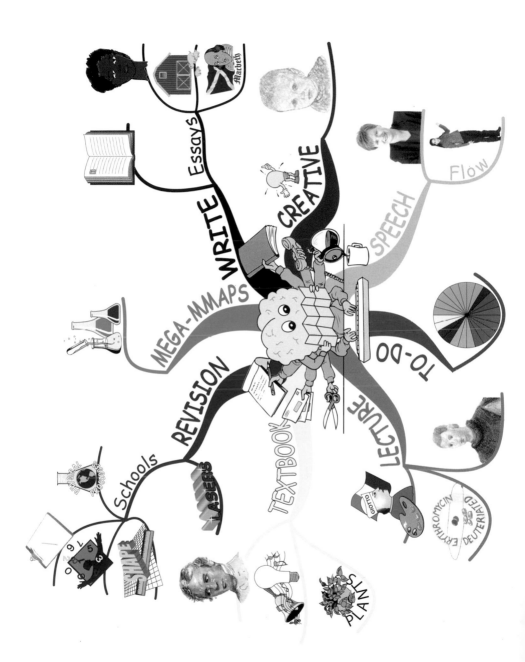

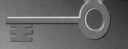

WRITING A BOOK

Using a Mind Map to plan the structure and content of a book before actually writing the text has a number of advantages.

- You know what you ve covered and what you have still got to cover.

- You can write bits out of sequence without losing the overall flow of the entire book.

- It gives many people the ability to work on different bits of the book simultaneously.

- You can create the easier bits first before going on to the more difficult bits.

- You can create the book as a whole as opposed to a series of bits.

The majority of this book was written in two weeks using the Mind Map on the next page as a guide.

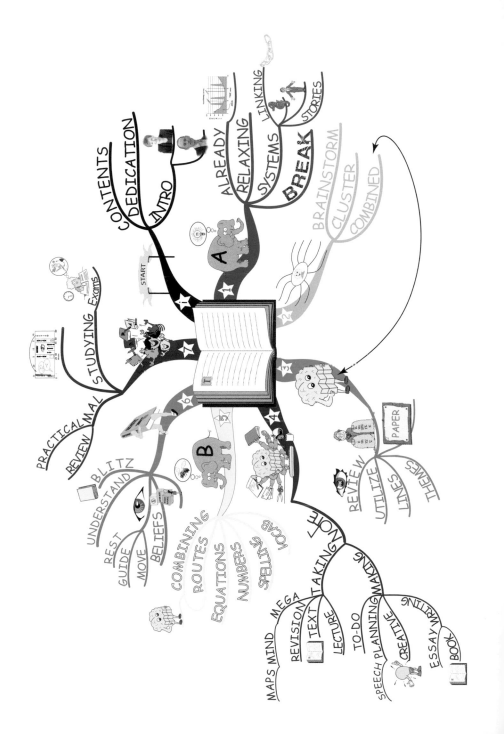

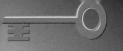

AN ESSAY PLAN

The structure of a Mind Map shows inherent logic – ideal as an essay plan.

- Begin writing at 2 o clock and work around the Mind Map step by step.

- Main themes, followed by argument, followed by evidence – footnotes. Repeat through each branch.

- Easy to give an overview, review and summary conclusions of your essay.

- Nothing goes adrift because of the logical progression of ideas.

- Your own associations shown by arrows on the Mind Map are those which earn you additional marks in essays – showing that you have understood the information and can connect it to other info that you have learned in different subject areas.

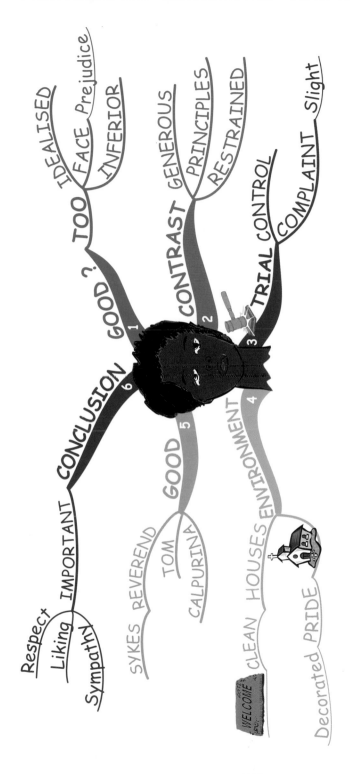

From an original Mind Map by Anne Jones preparing
to write an essay answering the question:
"What do you think about presentation of the black characters in
'To Kill a Mockingbird'?"

49

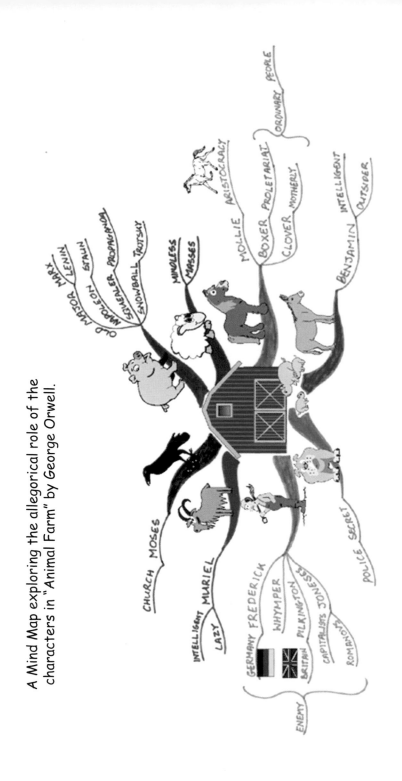

A Mind Map exploring the allegorical role of the characters in "Animal Farm" by George Orwell.

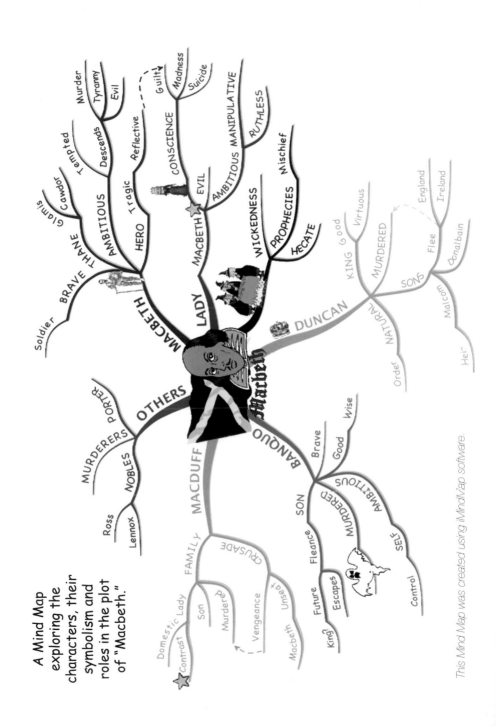

A Mind Map exploring the characters, their symbolism and roles in the plot of "Macbeth."

Macbeth

MACBETH
- BRAVE
  - THANE
    - Glamis
    - Cawdor
  - Soldier
- AMBITIOUS
  - Tempted
  - Descends
  - Tragic
- HERO
  - Reflective
- CONSCIENCE
  - Guilt
  - Madness
  - Suicide

MACBETH
- EVIL
  - AMBITIOUS
  - MANIPULATIVE
    - RUTHLESS

LADY
- WICKEDNESS
  - PROPHECIES
    - Mischief
  - HECATE

DUNCAN
- KING Good
  - Virtuous
- MURDERED
  - SONS
    - Flee
      - England
      - Ireland
    - Malcolm
    - Donalbain
    - Heir
- NATURAL
  - Order

OTHERS
- MURDERERS
- PORTER
- NOBLES
  - Ross
  - Lennox

MACDUFF
- FAMILY
  - Domestic Lady
    - Contrast
  - Son
  - Murdered
- CRUSADE
  - Vengeance
  - Unseat
    - Macbeth

BANQUO
- Brave
- Good
- Wise
- SON
  - Fleance
    - Future
    - King?
    - Escapes
- AMBITIOUS
  - MURDERED
  - SELF
    - Control

This Mind Map was created using MindMap software.

CREATIVE MIND MAPS

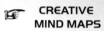
Creativity is largely to do with making new and novel connections and associations. Since a Mind Map is a network of connections, it is naturally suited to stimulate and support creative thoughts.

Creative Mind Maps differ from Study Mind Maps in several ways:

• You do not have to restrict yourself to 7±2 branches. You are not aiming to remember the information on the Mind Map in the first instance. It is merely to capture thoughts. You can produce a second, refined Mind Map later.

• Suspend judegment. To be truly creative you must be prepared to break outside the conventional. One way of doing this is to record absurd or stupid thoughts that may lead to a new perspective.

• Use as many pictures as possible. These can stimulate ideas more widely than words.

• If you find yourself running out of ideas, add an extra branch with nothing on it. The brain likes completion and will generate additional ideas to fill empty branches.

A creative Mind Map of Elaine's hopes and dreams for her son, James.

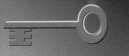

PLANNING A SPEECH

Mind Maps are a great way of organising your thoughts when planning a speech or presentation.

Try the following process:

- Brainstorm what you already know about the topic (see chapter 2).

- Cluster the information into categories.

- Decide on the content you want to include, discard irrelevant points, identify areas that need research - find appropriate sources.

- Create a first draft Mind Map, adding relevant research data as appropriate.

- Decide on the sequence of the presentation using a story-board.

- Create the final Mind Map.

- Prepare visual aids and handouts.

- Create a memory route with the main points and review (see chapter 5).

- When you give the speech you only need the single page Mind Map with its keywords as prompts. You may even find that you can remember the content without referring to your Mind Map!

This is a Mind Map planning a whole day seminar that Elaine gave to a group of teachers and learning support staff. You should be able to recognise a lot of the content, as it is similar to what we explain in this book.

Steps to plan and deliver a presentation

Brainstorm
as many ideas
as you can

Cluster
related ideas

Mind Map

Story-board
to sequence

Prepare visual
aids and handouts

Route main points

Edit, select, reject
& research

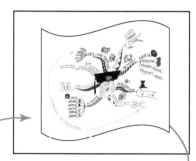

Final Mind Map
of presentation

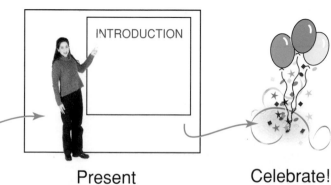

INTRODUCTION

Present

Celebrate!

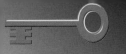

A TO-DO 'LIST'

Mind Maps can be very useful for managing your time on a daily, weekly or monthly basis.

Because the structure of a Mind Map lets you summarise everything on a a singe page, you can immediately see connections and relationships that you might not otherwise have realised. For example, if something you need to do relies on getting information from someone else, this can be indicated by an arrow or code.

Another advantage of using Mind Maps as to-do lists is that they are more memorable. Even without frequent review, you are more likely to remember a colourful, image rich Mind Map than a single colour, linear list.

Once you have completed a task shown on your Mind Map, use a highlighter pen to strike off the relevant branch. This gives a good visual indication of what s done and what s still to do.

In the example on the next page we divided a circle into 24 sectors to represent 24 hours of a day. Then we colour coded them according to the planned activity that is described on the corresponding branches.

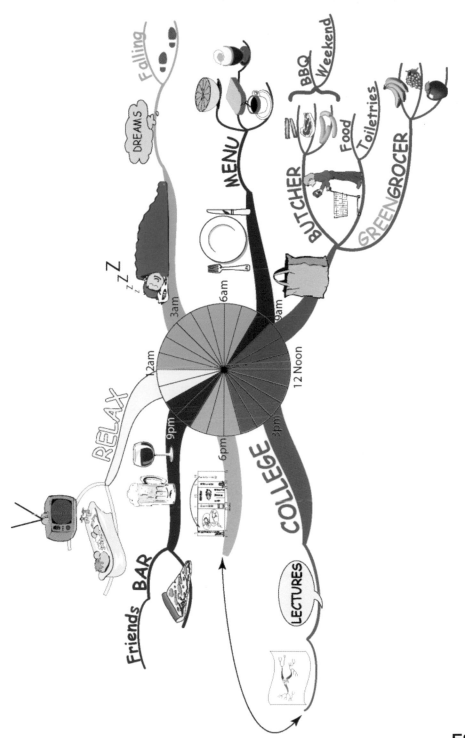

59

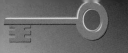

LECTURE NOTES

This is one of the most difficult Mind Maps to create as you tend to be doing it in live time.

Try practising on something not involved in your studies until you are confident of your ability to keep up. We suggest you try Mind Mapping parts of the TV news or something similar.

You are only trying to capture between 5 and 10% of the presented words. At the end of lecture this will be even less as your lecturer summarises, repeats or reviews the information covered.

To make it easier to Mind Map lectures on a regular basis, create a habit where you ask the lecturer in advance for the main topic and themes to be covered. You can then be one jump ahead by creating a unique central image and main branches before you even go into the lecture. This will leave you plenty of time to spend creating a beautifully creative and memorable Mind Map.

A Mind Map of a lecture on the life and
work of the painter Giotto.

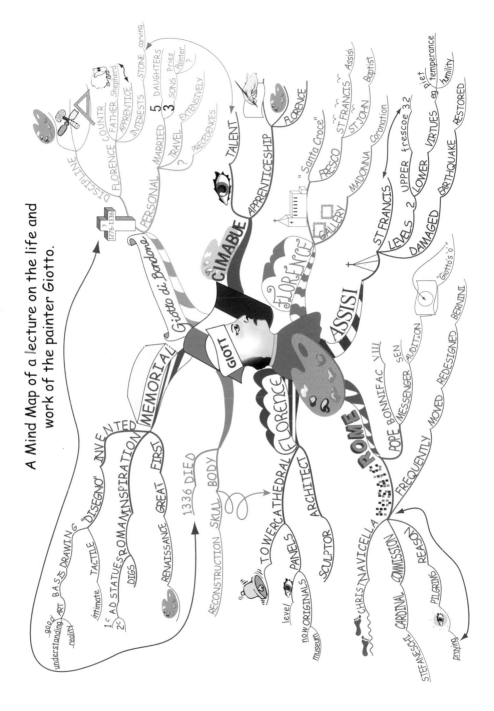

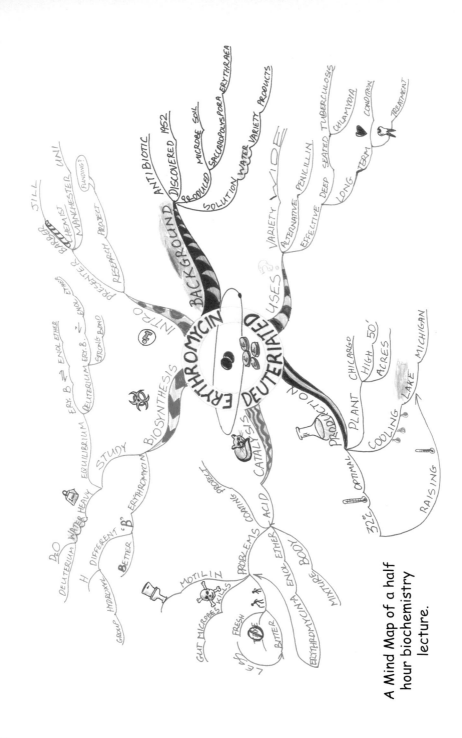

A Mind Map of a half hour biochemistry lecture.

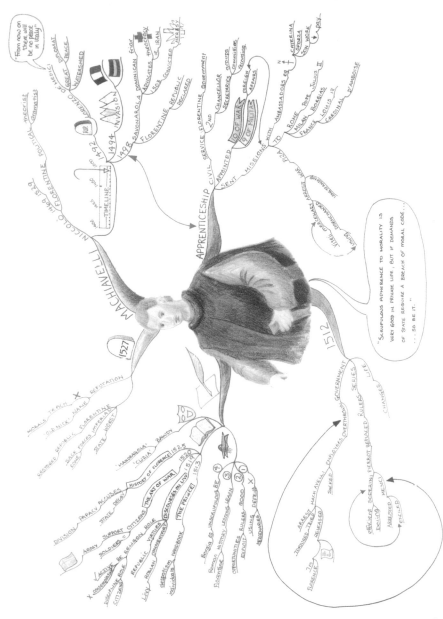

A Mind Map
of a lecture
on the life
of Machiavelli.

NOTES FROM A TEXT BOOK (KEYWORDS)

Finding the keywords from a piece of written or spoken text is often thought to be the most difficult skill to acquire in Mind Mapping.

Keywords tend to be nouns and may only make up between 5 and 10% of the text being presented. They are easily identified as being the most important words or themes within that text.

You can make the words easy to find by highlighting them in your book or notes before you begin to Mind Map.

On this page we have identified the keywords for you and presented them in the portion of a Mind Map below…

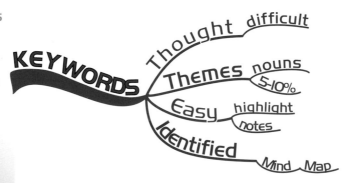

The example on the next page is a Mind Map of a whole chapter from a text book.

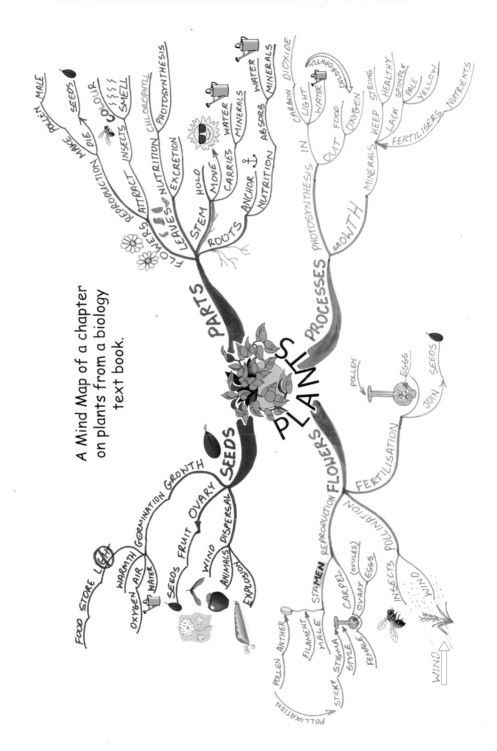

A Mind Map of a chapter on plants from a biology text book.

65

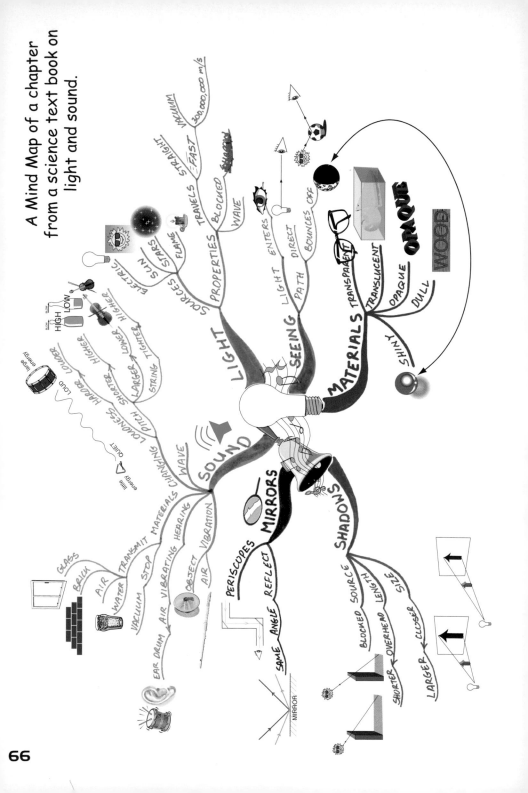

A Mind Map of a chapter from a science text book on light and sound.

66

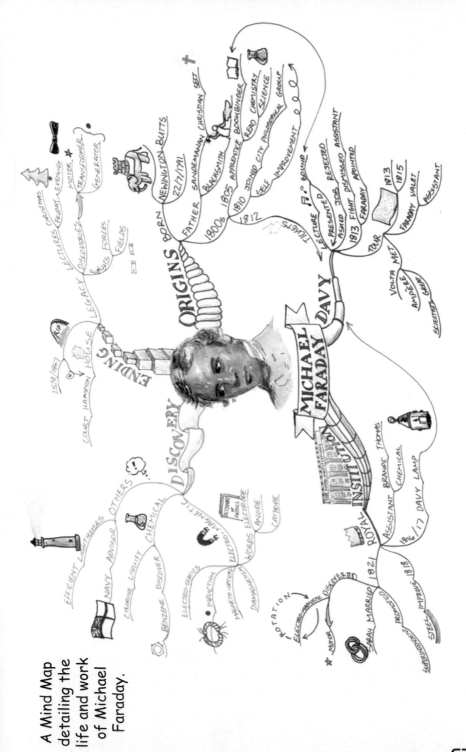

A Mind Map detailing the life and work of Michael Faraday.

CURRICULUM REVISION

Using Mind Mapping as a revision aid has two main advantages:

- You can see an overview of whole curriculum. This puts everything into its logical place.

- Mind Maps can be used for review. You can highlight branches as you finish your 5 times review.

Practice redrawing the Mind Map from memory. When you can do this you will never again be stumped for an answer in an exam. Simply redraw the Mind Map and begin your answer.

Review with friends by photocopying your Mind Map in black and white. Read the Mind Map to them to help them understand your associations. If they colour in the Mind Map as you share it and add their own images, codes and associations it will make the Mind Map personal to them and easier to remember.

Even better: Divide your curriculum by 5 and recruit 4 friends to produce a Mind Map of their section. You can all cover the entire curriculum in 20% of the time. The most difficult thing will be figuring out what to do with all your free time...

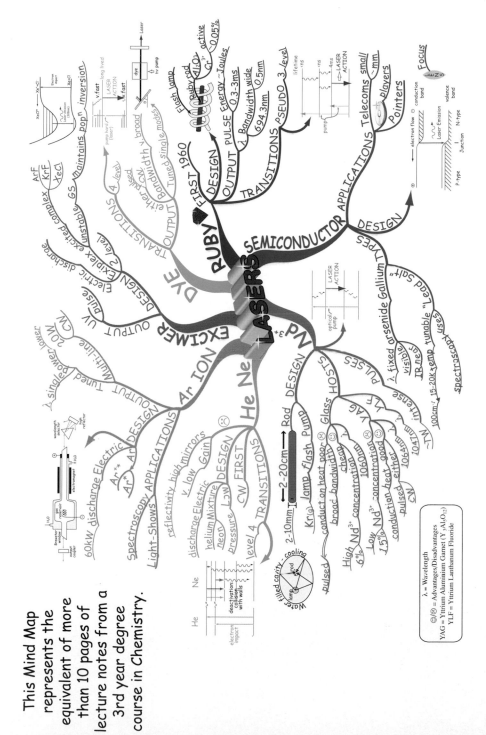

This Mind Map represents the equivalent of more than 10 pages of lecture notes from a 3rd year degree course in Chemistry.

λ = Wavelength
☺/☹ = Advantages/Disadvantages
YAG = Yttrium Aluminium Garnet ($Y_3Al_5O_{12}$)
YLF = Yttrium Lanthanum Fluoride

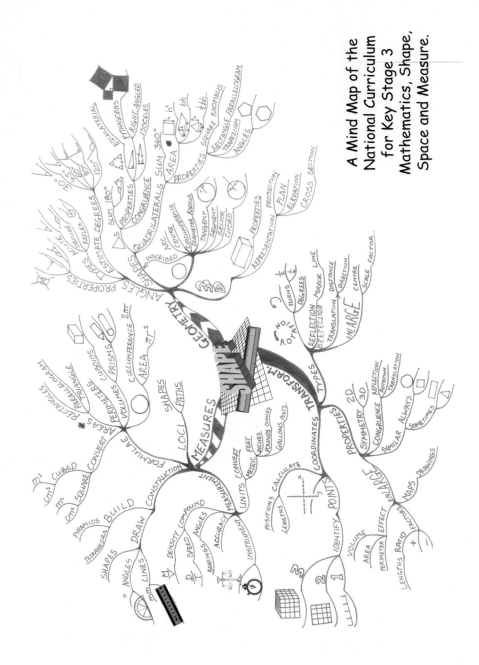

A Mind Map of the National Curriculum for Key Stage 3 Mathematics, Shape, Space and Measure.

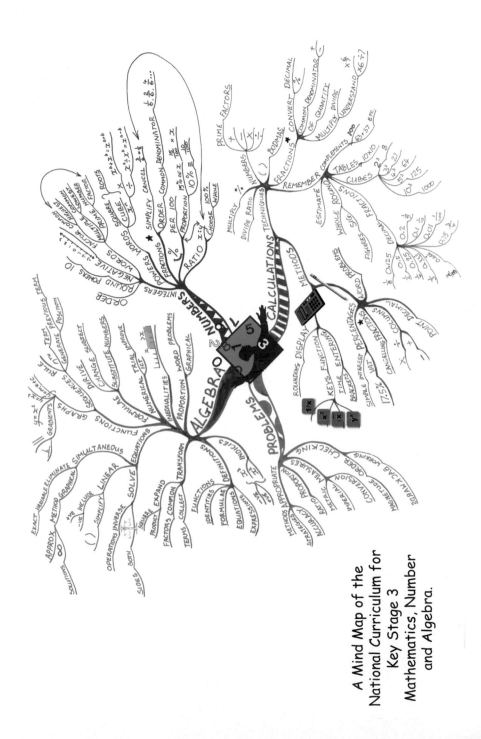

A Mind Map of the
National Curriculum for
Key Stage 3
Mathematics, Number
and Algebra.

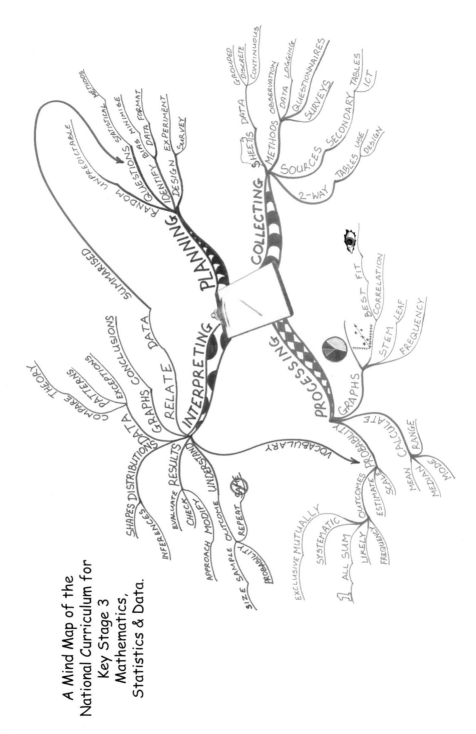

A Mind Map of the
National Curriculum for
Key Stage 3
Mathematics,
Statistics & Data.

PLANNING

RANDOM UNPREDICTABLE
STATISTICAL METHODS
QUESTIONS MINIMISE
IDENTIFY BIAS DATA FORMAT
DESIGN EXPERIMENT
SURVEY

COLLECTING

GROUPED
DISCRETE
CONTINUOUS
DATA LOGGING
OBSERVATION
QUESTIONNAIRES
METHODS
SHEETS DATA
SURVEYS
SECONDARY TABLES
ICT
SOURCES
TABLES USE
DESIGN
2-WAY

SUMMARISED

PROCESSING

BEST FIT
CORRELATION
STEM LEAF
FREQUENCY
GRAPHS
VOCABULARY
CALCULATE
RANGE
MEAN
MEDIAN
MODE
PROBABILITY
SCALE ESTIMATE
OUTCOMES
LIKELY
FREQUENCY
ALL SUM
SYSTEMATIC
EXCLUSIVE MUTUALLY

INTERPRETING

RELATE DATA
GRAPHS
CONCLUSIONS
DATA EXCEPTIONS
DISTRIBUTIONS PATTERNS
SHAPES
COMPARE THEORY
INFERENCES
RESULTS
CHECK EVALUATE
MODIFY UNDERSTAND
APPROACH OUTCOME
REPEAT SIZE
SIZE SAMPLE
PROBABILITY

72

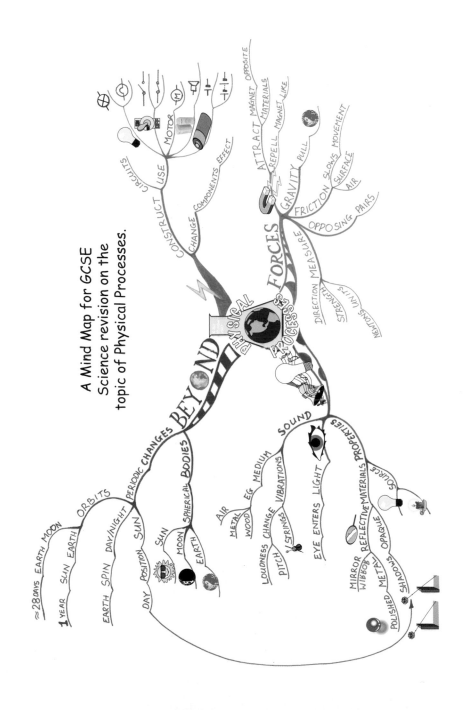

A Mind Map for GCSE Science revision on the topic of Physical Processes.

MEGA MIND MAPS

Imagine you have a map of the world. It has countries and major cities labeled.

If you now look at a map of Britain, you see more detail: Motorways, towns, cities, main railway lines and major rivers.

Now take a road atlas. You see all the roads, villages, places of interest, etc.

Mind Maps are just the same. Notes from lectures or books are like the road atlas maps, containing lots of important detail but not easily placed in context. Curriculum revision Mind Maps may be a little less detailed and sum up the contents of a whole lecture on just one branch.

A Mega Mind Map is your map of the world. It covers an entire year s study on a single sheet of paper (At least A2 size, up to A0). Pin your Mega Mind Map to your wall and review it regularly. It won t contain all the detail of the course but will help you to identify the themes that run through it. By seeing, literally, the big picture, you can make the connections that distinguish a B+ student from an A or A+.

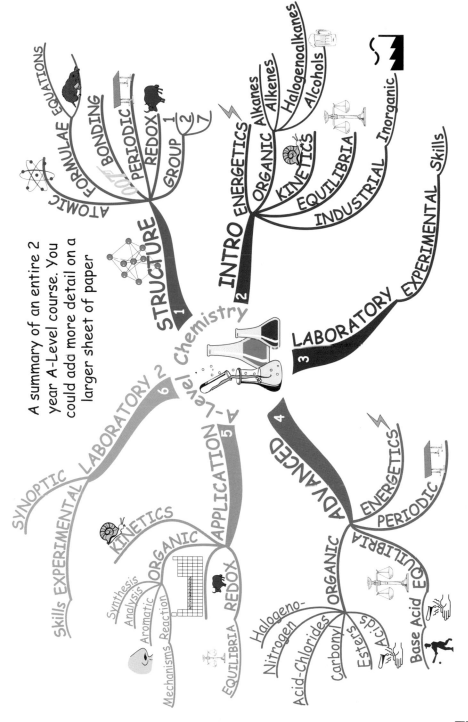

A summary of an entire 2 year A-Level course. You could add more detail on a larger sheet of paper

A-Level Chemistry

STRUCTURE 1
- ATOMIC
- FORMULAE EQUATIONS
- BONDING
- PERIODIC
- REDOX
- GROUP 1 2 7

INTRO 2
- ENERGETICS
- ORGANIC
  - Alkanes
  - Alkenes
  - Halogenoalkanes
  - Alcohols
- KINETICS
- EQUILIBRIA
- INDUSTRIAL Inorganic

LABORATORY 3
- EXPERIMENTAL Skills

ADVANCED 4
- ENERGETICS
- PERIODIC
- EQUILIBRIA
  - Acid Base
- ORGANIC
  - Acids
  - Esters
  - Carbonyl
  - Acid-Chlorides
  - Halogeno-
  - Nitrogen
- REDOX
- EQUILIBRIA

APPLICATION 5
- KINETICS
- ORGANIC
  - Synthesis
  - Analysis
  - Aromatic
  - Mechanisms Reaction

LABORATORY 6
- EXPERIMENTAL Skills
- SYNOPTIC

75

CHAPTER FIVE

MEMORY PART B

INTRODUCTION

You should by now be comfortable using some of the simpler memory systems such as the **Body List**, the **Link System** and using your ability to create strong memories by creating images using the **SEAHORSE** principles…

We will now show you some of the systems used by the world s greatest Memory Champions. These are not systems that are similar to the ones they use, but **exactly** the same. They just use them for recalling much larger chunks of information than you will need at the moment. To pass exams you need to be able to run for a bus. World Champions in the memory field need to be able to run marathons in record breaking times. Don t get disheartened if you feel you still have a huge way to go to get to where the champions are. By using the systems in this book you will still be better informed and studying more efficiently than the majority of students around the planet.

The route system that we will learn about in this section is a more advanced version of the **Body List**, but instead of memorising ten bits of information, what you can memorise is limited only by your imagination.

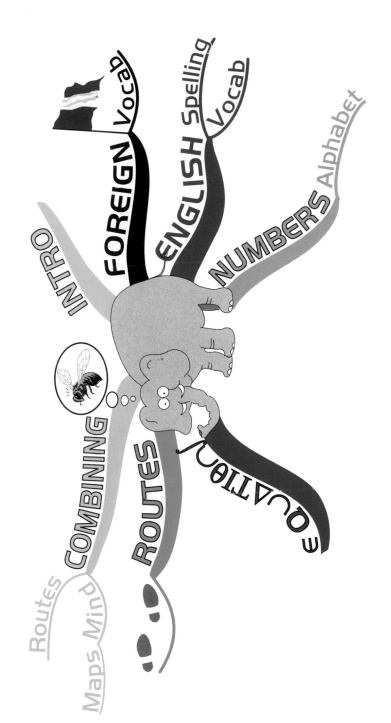

FOREIGN VOCABULARY

Learning foreign language vocabulary is often a challenge for students struggling to associate the new word to something they already know.

To make this process easier, try linking each English word with its French equivalent by creating imaginary pictures or situations. If you apply the **SEAHORSE** principles and take care to use a situation or picture in which the link word closely matches the correct French pronunciation you will find your recall is greatly enhanced.

The more fun you have creating memorable imaginary pictures the easier they will be to recall, but you can also increase your recall by capturing your images in Mind Map form and following the suggested review process of 10 minutes, 1 day, 1 week, 1 month and three months. A large vocabulary in your Long term Memory will make it easier to locate the correct word when you are writing or speaking the new language.

For Example:

1. The French for **BREAD** is PAIN
   (pronounced PAHN)

Imagine that you are cramming
hundreds of French bread sticks into
a pan and are jumping up and down
on top of the lid to try and get it to fit.

2. The French for **WINE** is VIN
   (pronounced VAHN)

Imagine standing in a street feeling
very, very thirsty. You yank open the
rear door of a massive white van
and thousands of bottles of wine
cascade from the back, shattering
on the road and swamping you in a
pool of fruity smelling wine.

3. The French for **MENU** is CARTE
   (pronounced KART)

You are trying to order in a
restaurant – your waiters are riding
around in little go–carts and every
time they whiz past your table you
make a frantic effort to try and reach
out and grab a menu from one of
them.

SPELLING

Successful spellers generally see words rather than hearing them in their head. English is often being taught using phonics such as d - o - g . This is a good strategy for learning to read but the most commonly misspelled words are those that don t follow phonetic rules.

The position of a person s eyes when thinking can reveal whether they are seeing a mental picture, hearing a sound or expereincing a feeling. They will generally look up and to their left to recall pictures. This position in space is where most people naturally file images. So it makes sense to put mental images of words that you want to learn in the same place.

To remember the spelling of a word, write the word clearly on a piece of card and hold it up to the top left of your field of view. Carefully look at the word, noticing its shape. Then put down the card and see the word in your imagination. Try varying aspects of the mental image to make it more memorable. Change colours, brightness, perhaps even make it flash.

When you need to recall a word s spelling just look up and to your left. With practice you can simply read off the spelling in your mind s eye.

Vocabulary Building

You can learn English vocabulary in the same way as learning foreign vocabulary.
Just make a mental picture that relates the word to its meaning.

For example:

Pogonophobia - Fear of beards.
Associate a bearded man on a pogo stick.

Coelacanth - An African sea fish previously thought to be extinct.
Associate a Sealer can with a fish in it.

Terrarium - A place for keeping small land animals.
Associate a terrapin in a tank.

Most scientific or medical terms have Latin or Greek origins. Once you know a prefix or suffix you can easily associate a number of similarly derived words, making it easier to rapidly build your vocabulary.

You learned Terrarium . Terra is Latin for earth so you can now guess the meaning of:

Terrestrial, Terraform, Extraterrestrial, Terra Firma

Next time you find a word you don t understand, make an association to the meaning and use the spelling system.

83

NUMBERS

Numbers are abstract concepts. They are hard to memorise because memories are pictures and abstract concepts are not.

To make memorising simpler all you have to do is represent the number as a picture of an object. One way to do this is to use the following code where each number is represented by a letter contained within a phonetic alphabet.

"In order for you to learn the method, you must first learn a simple phonetic alphabet…. With a different consonant sound for each of the digits. I'll make this simple for you by giving you a 'memory aid' for remembering each

Harry Lorayne
Memory Pioneer

No. Sound Memory aid

0 s or z first sound of the word 'zero'
1 d or T both have only one downstroke
2 n written 'n' has two downstrokes
3 m written 'm' has three downstrokes
4 r last sound of the word 'four'
5 l Roman numeral for 50 is 'L'
6 g letter 'g' turned around looks like 6
7 k two 7's together form a 'K'
8 f handwritten 'f' (𝒻) looks like an 8
9 b or p number 9 turned around is like 'b' or 'p'

By taking pairs of numbers from the number you wish to remember and substituting letters you can create words by adding vowels which you can then string together into a link system, as you did earlier with the Periodic Table.

Eg. To remember the number pi: $\pi \approx 3.14159$

3.1   =   m t   =   mat

41   =   r t   =   rat

59   =   l b   =   lab

Imagine a welcome mat placed
outside your chemistry classroom where a giant rat
is demonstrating a practical lab experiment and who
throws a custard pie in your face.

EQUATIONS

We use a similar method to make equations more memorable by turning them into pictures.

These pictures can again be remembered by using the link system and the **SEAHORSE** principles or combined with the route technique that we will look at next…

For example, a particularly useful but hard to remember equation (if you re not using a technique) is the formula for solving quadratic equations:

Where: $ax^2 + bx + c = 0$

$$x = \frac{-b \pm \sqrt{b^2 - 4ac}}{2a}$$

We can associate each symbol in turn with a picture related to it by either the same sound or a rhyme.

x   x-ray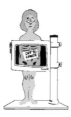

=   eagle

-     Midas (gold)

b   bee

and so on…

So the beginning of the 'link' story reads:

"Imagine you're x-raying an eagle. Inside his chest is a pot of gold but covered in honey being collected by thousands of bees."

THE ROUTE SYSTEM

This is one of the oldest recorded memory systems, used by the Ancient Greeks and Romans. As the capacity of our brains has not changed significantly in the last 2,500 years, what they did then is still as applicable today.

Routes work on the same basis as the **Body List**. You create an image of the information you wish to remember. Instead of linking the image to a location on your body. Associate it with a place along a very familiar journey or route.

Think of a route or journey that you know well and can travel along in your imagination. As you take the journey there will be a series of places or landmarks that you pass along the way. These will always be the same whenever you take the journey and will always be passed in the same order. These loci are used as hooks on which to hang the information to be remembered.

For example your landmarks could be:

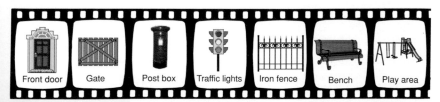

Front door | Gate | Post box | Traffic lights | Iron fence | Bench | Play area

Whilst you can easily use outside routes to hang your information on, the method I used to study for five A-Levels was to use a different room in my house for each subject. I used my bedroom for Biology, the living-room for English and the hall for Art History.

Here's an example of one of the routes I used:

There are lots of locations around the room, these can be as small as the light switch or as large as the wardrobe.

I imagined an object symbolising a different aspect of biology in each place: jeans for genetics, a plant for photosynthesis, a plate of sandwiches for digestion, etc.

Remember to use
S
E
A
H
O
R
S
E

THE ROUTE SYSTEM
SUMMARY

○ Prepare in your mind a well known route.

○ Select locations along your route in the order you come across them.

○ Using the **SEAHORSE** principles, create an image of the information you need to remember.

○ Attach the image to each location in order along your route.

○ Review your route thoroughly. You ll soon find that you are able to remember your information forwards and backwards, by travelling both ways along your route.

You can also learn to combine the Route techniques with other systems such as Mind Mapping. You can either place Mind Maps along your routes, or routes on to your Mind Maps.

ROUTES ON MIND MAPS

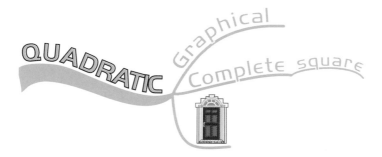

You create your Mind Map as usual adding the various aspects of theory on the branches. You then add another branch on which you draw the first location along your route where you have recorded data related to the theory (e.g. in our example the front door is the first location used to store the formula for solving quadratic equations).

When you come to review your Mind Map, you will see the picture of the front door and run through the route in your imagination before moving on to the next branch.

MIND MAPS AND ROUTES

When Mind Mapping, you are encouraged to create a unique 'Central Image' to help you remember the Mind Map after your 5-times review. By setting up a route to use for each subject, I was able to associate the central image to a place on my route. Recalling the location with the central image from the Mind Map placed in it would then allow me to easily recreate the whole Mind Map in my imagination.

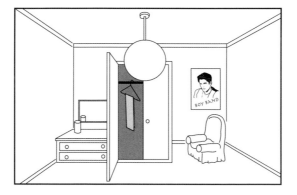

The central image of a pair of faded denim jeans (Genetics) was associated to my wardrobe. In my imagination, I could open the door of my wardrobe, see the faded jeans hanging up and thus recall the Genetics Mind Map.

CHAPTER SIX

SPEED READING

SPEED READING

INTRODUCTION

In this section we will look at speed reading...

We will give you a variety of techniques, not only to help you read faster, but also to help you read smarter!

By reading smarter we mean boosting understanding, finding and remembering the key points and, with the help of your friends, multiplying your effectiveness many times over.

"Learning
to speed read effortlessly
and fluently has been claimed by
millions of people around the world to
be one of the most rewarding and
significant events of
their lives."

Tony Buzan
The Speed Reading Book

94

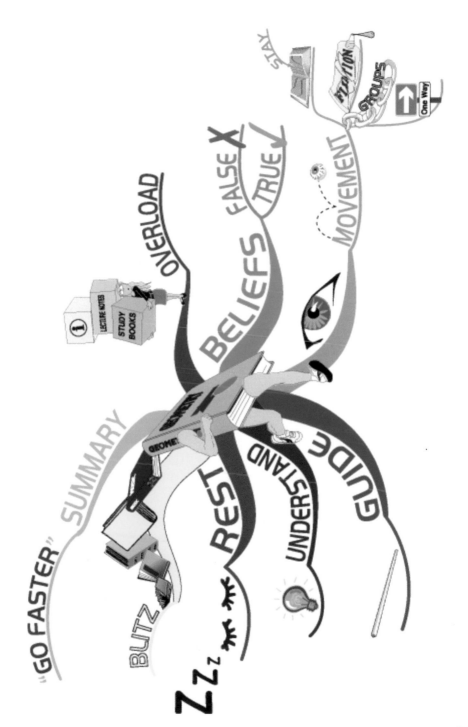

INFORMATION OVERLOAD

How many books do you have on your reading list?

Be honest. How many have you *ACTUALLY* read?

How do you know what s worth reading until you ve read it?

Wouldn't it be great if you could read a book in an afternoon?

Or even better...
get someone else to read the books for you and tell you the important bits?

Do you know...

About 1,000 books are published internationally every day and the total of all printed knowledge doubles every five years.

Then there are reports, newspapers, magazines, journals, plus the massive explosion of material on the World Wide Web.

So how fast do I need to read to cope with this?

The average reading speed is between 150 words per minute and 240 words per minute.

The United Nations stated that to keep pace with all this information you would need to read at 400 wpm (but this was before the advent of e-mail, the Internet and texting).

An easy target to aim for is 1,000 words per minute. However, with practice you can actually read at over 3,000 wpm.

BELIEFS

Have you ever been told...

✗ Saying the words under your breath slows you down.

✓ *Saying words under your breath can help you remember - especially if you mentally shout out important bits.*

✗ Pointing at words with your finger is childish.

✓ *As we'll see later, finger pointing dramatically increases speed.*

✗ Read "slowly and carefully".

✓ *Reading quickly can increase your understanding.*

✗ Begin at the beginning and go through to the end.

✓ *You can learn more by just picking out important stuff from a book.*

✗ Go back and reread or look up anything you don't understand before you carry on.

✓ *Interrupting your flow reduces understanding and slows you down.*

✗ Read one word at a time.

✓ *You can easily read several words at a time.*

✗ You should understand everything you read.

✓ *100% comprehension is hardly ever necessary.*

✗ You can only read what your eyes are focusing on.

✓ *You can see an entire page with a single glance and take in more than you may think.*

✗ Never write on books.

✓ *A good way to engage with a book is to highlight words and make notes in the margins.*

Anne Jones has won the Mind Sports Olympiad reading tournament six times in a row.

What's more, she only uses the techniques that we'll show you!

THE EYES

A typical reader s eyes move something like this when they read a piece of text…

Jumping from word to word resting on each,

sometimes they skip backwards,

or even wonder off the page completely.

The way to speed up your reading is to avoid all these bad habits. Let us explain…

GROUPS OF WORDS

If you take in groups of words at a time instead of reading the words one by one you can greatly increase your speed. Even if you only took in two at a time, that would double your speed and it s possible to take in six or more!

FIXATION TIME

A fixation is the name given to the stops in-between jumps when the eye recognises each word (or group of words). These last for anything between a quarter and one and a half seconds. If you can halve the time each fixation takes you can double your speed again!

ONLY GOING FORWARDS

Every time you back skip you waste time. So make an effort to only move forwards.

STAY ON THE PAGE

This sounds obvious, but by keeping your attention on the page and not allowing your eyes and thoughts to wander, you can improve your speed still further.

On the next page we'll give you a technique to help you to do all these things…

GUIDES

When you learned to read you probably used your finger to point to the words as you read them.

It was a good technique and worked very well until one day your teacher said something like, "Now you know how to read take your finger off the page because pointing at the words slows you down."

Surely a better thing to have done would have been to move your finger faster!

Your eyes are designed to follow moving objects. When you catch a ball, you don t see lots of static images. Your eyes follow and track it and help you move you hands into the right position (hopefully) to catch it.

Your eyes can move much more smoothly if they have something to follow. This could be your finger, a pencil or a chopstick. The benefit of a long slender guide is that it doesn t cover up what s coming next so you can see a preview of text up ahead before you actually read it.

The really great thing about using a guide is that it helps you apply the other techniques that we have just talked about:

GROUPS OF WORDS

By starting a little way in from the left and stopping a little way in from the right you are forcing your eyes to take in groups of words at the start and the end of lines.

FIXATION TIME

The faster you move the guide, the shorter your fixation times will be.

ONLY GOING FORWARDS

You don t have to be a genius for this one!

STAY ON THE PAGE

Keep your guide on the page and keep your eyes on your guide.

 THINGS TO AVOID

Don t tap out words as you read them - move your guide in a smooth flowing motion under the words.

Don t use your guide like a ruler as this stops you seeing what s coming up. Instead use it as a pointer, so your eye follows the tip.

UNDERSTANDING

No matter how fast you read, if you don't understand any of it then there isn't any point in reading it!

One of the benefits of speeding up is that you can actually improve your understanding.

Every word or idea can be the starting point for the brain to make lots of associations. If you read too slowly then you are giving your brain plenty of time to make many associations, most of which will have nothing to do with the text. The faster you go the closer you are to understanding the author's intent and associations!

Another way to boost understanding is to re-read the text. If you re reading at twice your usual speed, you can read the text twice in the same amount of time.

Try not to make re-reading a habit though. It not only defeats one of the reasons for speed reading - to free up more of your time - but also reduces your concentration. World Memory Champion, Dominic O Brien explains...

"In my act I memorise words called out by the audience. In theory, the longer I take, the clearer the image and so the stronger the memory, but if there s too long a gap between words it throws my concentration. Because I know I m only going to hear each word once, it forces me to focus my mind more...

Likewise, when reading, by speeding up you get into a rhythm which aids concentration and so increases understanding. Tell yourself that you re only going to read each sentence once, otherwise you re telling your mind that it doesn t have to focus so hard the first time."

INTRODUCTION

INFORMATION
OVERLOAD

BELIEFS

GUIDES

UNDERSTANDING

R&R FOR
THE RETINA

BOOK BLITZ

SUMMARY

R&R FOR THE RETINA
RESTING THE EYES

Just like any other muscle the eyes need rest, especially when you have been reading or studying for a long while.

To refresh your eyes...

Rub your hands together briskly, until the palms are quite warm.

Lean forward on your elbows, cupping your hands over your closed eyes, resting lightly.

Think of blackness: black velvet, a black cat, a deep, dark, moonless night.

Rest like this for at least one minute.

Open your eyes and feel refreshed!

RADIANT READING

"Where shall I begin, please your Majesty? he asked. Begin at the beginning, said the King, gravely, and go on till you come to the end: then stop."

Lewis Carroll
Alice in Wonderland

This advice may have been the best available in 1865 when Lewis Carroll wrote "Alice in Wonderland."

We now know that the best way to get the information from a book, especially a text book, isn t to read from beginning to end. Instead, work from the sections, to the chapters, to the headings in the text, to the details.

We ll show you how in the Book Blitz on the next page…

BOOK BLITZ

With a group of friends
select a book each

Look at the cover of your book

Sections become main
branches

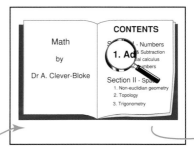

Find the chapters of the book

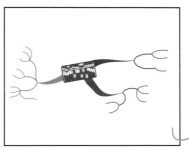

These become third
level branches

Speed Read the rest of
the text.

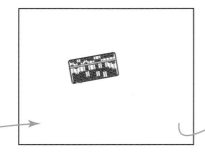

Decide on a central image

Find the sections of the book

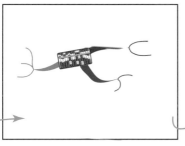

Chapters become
second level branches

In each chapter find any
headings in the text

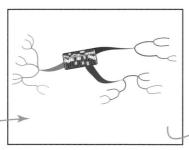

Add details

Copy Mind Maps and
share with friends
(each person explain theirs)

Celebrate

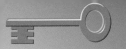

INTRODUCTION

INFORMATION
OVERLOAD

BELIEFS

GUIDES

UNDERSTANDING

R&R FOR
THE RETINA

BOOK BLITZ

SUMMARY

SUMMARY

The speed reading techniques can be summarised with the acronym
GO FASTER...

Guide

Using a guide allows the eyes to move in a smoother way and helps with the other techniques.

Only Forwards

Back skipping wastes time and should be avoided. If you think you missed something keep going. It is very likely that you will understand what was meant by the context or the same point will often be repeated later.

Fixations Shorter

The less time your eyes spend resting on each word (or group of words) the faster you will read.

Allow Information to Come to You

Imagine reading as being like a sponge soaking up information rather than having to go out to grab it. This makes the process easier and much less stressful.

Stay on the Page

Keep your focus on the page. If you have problems concentrating make sure you take regular breaks and remember to rest your eyes when you start to get tired.

Take in Groups of Words

Practice increasing the number of words that you take in one go. If you can currently manage two, try three. You should eventually be able to read up to about six words at a time.

Enjoy

Everything, including reading is easier if it s fun. If you re not enjoying it, your thoughts will be elsewhere and you won t remember what you have read. So why did you waste the time reading it!

Reason for Reading

Before you start reading, decide what you want to get out of the text. Are there specific questions you need answering? Once you have a purpose, your brain will alert you to what you need - the information will leap out at you.

CHAPTER SEVEN

SUPER STUDY SKILLS

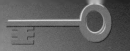

INTRODUCTION

In this section we will look at practical ways to apply what we know about how the brain works to successful studying.

You will see how quickly your brain can forget information and how to maintain high levels of recall through correct reviews.

This builds into an easy to follow, brain friendly review system that can be applied to all your studies.

Finally we'll show you how to draw together all the strategies in this book into a single plan for working towards exam success at any level.

MEMORY AFTER LEARNING

Normal students - even those with quite good grades still forget most of what they have learned within 24 hours. During that time they can lose 80-90% of the detail covered. Imagine, for every hour of study, they only remember about 10 minutes worth of information.

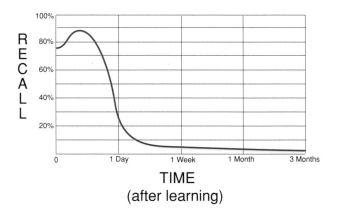

TIME
(after learning)

If you want to learn faster, work smarter and remember much more - here s how.

The easiest way to sustain your level of knowledge is to review it whilst your recall is at its peak. If you wait until your recall starts to decline then you have to relearn the information rather than merely review it.

Luckily this doesn't mean reviewing everything you have learned every day. Five reviews is enough to transfer your knowledge into long term memory. The ideal times to review are...

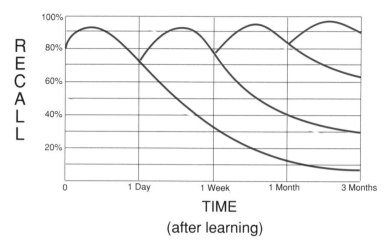

TIME
(after learning)

If you are using Mind Maps or one of the Memory Systems this entire review process can take less than 10 minutes in total. By starting to review as soon as you have learned something, you will never have to experience the panic of cramming at the last minute.

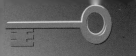

HOW TO REVISE

1   Take your notes in a memorable way (we suggest you use Mind Maps).

2   Date notes and add review codes:
       10 Minutes (10)
       Day (D)
       Week (W)
       Month (M)
       Three Months (3M).

3   Fold and punch Mind Maps for filing in your ring binder.

4   Name and number Mind Maps in sequence (eg Maths 1, Maths 2, etc).

5   File by subject.

6   Write the Mind Map name and number into your diary for review tomorrow.

7   Repeat for :

       1 week s time
       1 month s time
       3 months time.

8   On completion of each review strike through the appropriate review code on the bottom of each Mind Map.

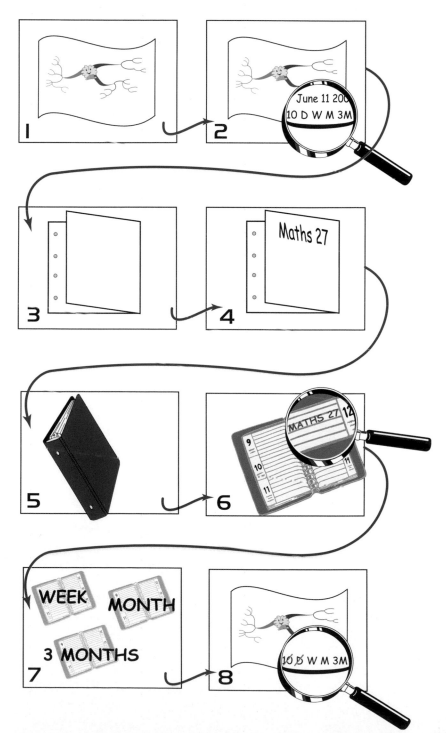

THE IDEAL
STUDY HOUR

Does it work?

Fourteen students from four South London schools approached us with a single burning ambition: "Show us what we need to get A s in our A-levels and we will do it" - and they did!

Despite three having dyslexia and one having cerebral palsy **ALL** passed their exams with flying colours - an amazing 42 A grades between them. Even more fantastic, one young lady decided to study for A-level Spanish with only six months to go before the exams "because learning was now so easy - I wanted a new challenge".

What did they do?

Exactly what you can learn to do here.

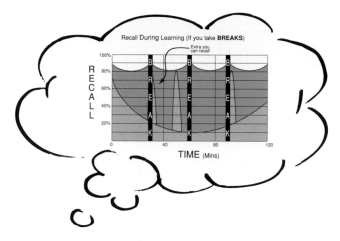

Recall During Learning (If you take **BREAKS**)

You can boost recall by taking breaks during your learning, so the Ideal Study System must include frequent breaks.

Do some gentle physical exercise in the first break to get better blood and oxygen flow to the brain

The body is about 90% water by volume so grab a drink (ideally water) in the second break.

In the third break practice your relaxation technique to be better prepared for exams.

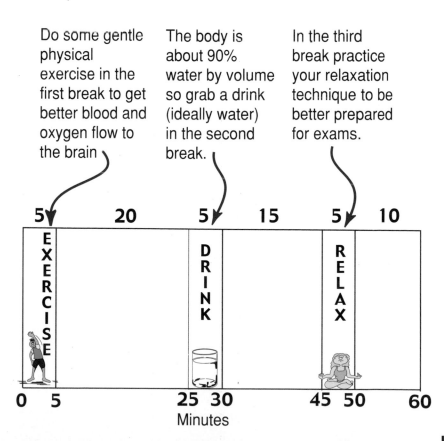

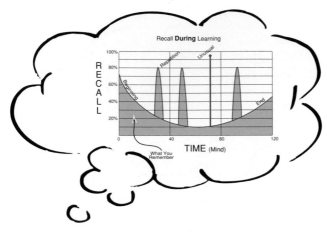

Spend the 20 minutes after your exercise using a study technique that works in harmony with your natural memory rhythms, ie lots of beginnings and ends, repeated and associated items and outstanding things.

Two examples of techniques that do this are Mind Mapping and the Route Memory System as both allow you to learn and recall large amounts of information easily..

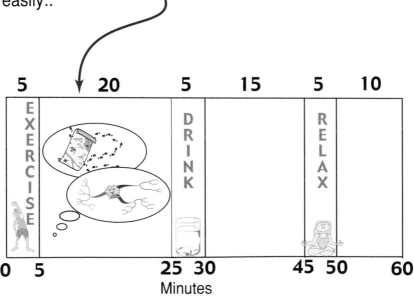

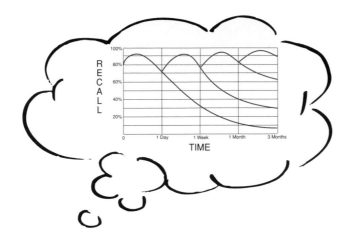

Spend the 15 minutes after your second break reviewing the Mind Maps or Routes from your files. Notes that you made yesterday, one week ago and one month ago. This won t take long, for example you can review a Mind Map in as little as 90 seconds.

"It's as important to review as to learn something new."

Linda Leckie
Student at LSE

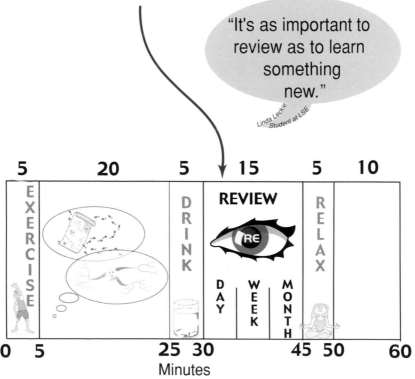

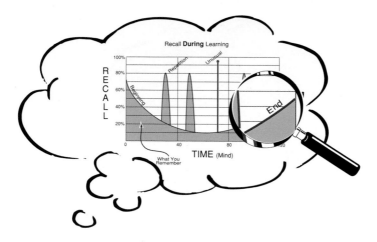

Because we recall more from the end of a session than from the middle the last 10 minutes is the ideal time for reviewing and completing the new work studied earlier. At this point you will see any gaps, additional connections or parts you do not yet understand.

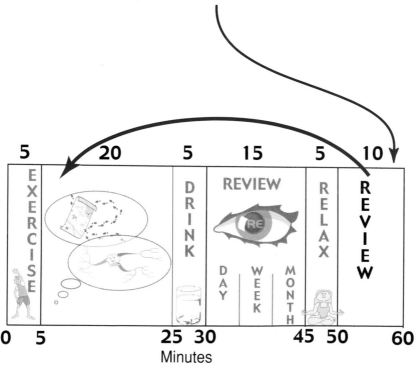

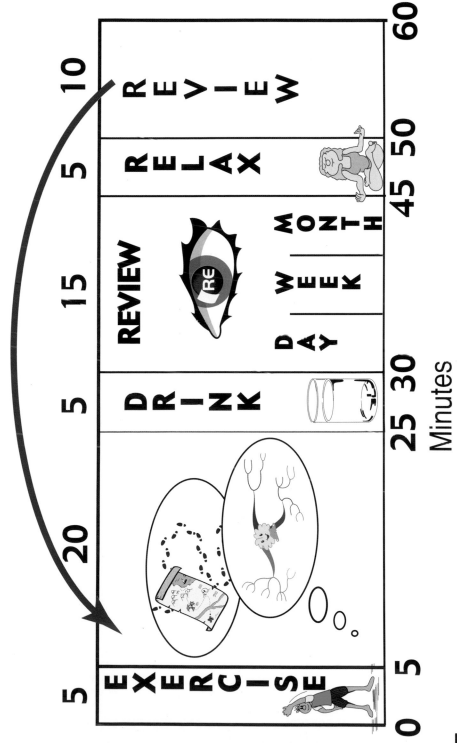

125

STUDYING FOR EXAMS

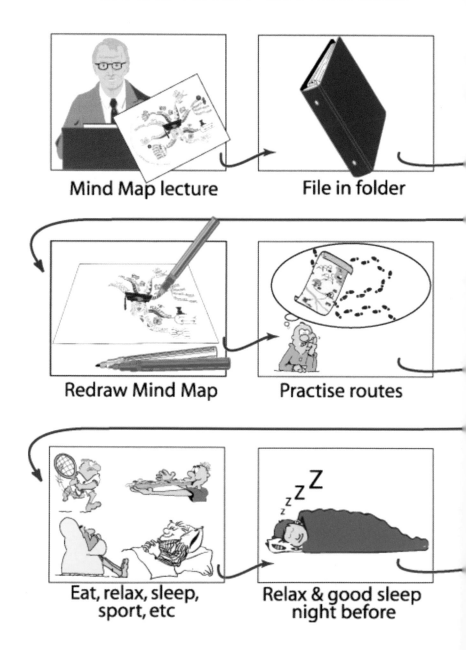

Mind Map lecture

File in folder

Redraw Mind Map

Practise routes

Eat, relax, sleep, sport, etc

Relax & good sleep night before

Review: 10 minutes
day, week, month, 3 months

Route main points

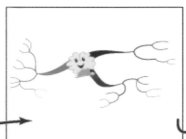

Create Mega Mind Map

Review Mega Mind Map
& routes daily

Exam

Celebrate

Further Reading

MEMORY
Buzan Bites: Brilliant Memory - Tony Buzan
ISBN 978-0-563-52033-7

How to Pass Exams – Dominic O'Brien
ISBN 978-1-84483-391-7

How to develop a Brilliant Memory - week by week
– Dominic O'Brien
ISBN 978-1-84483-153-1

Essential Lifeskills: Improving Your Memory - David Thomas
ISBN 978-0-7513-4895-8

MIND MAPPING
Buzan Bites: Mind Mapping - Tony Buzan
ISBN 978-0-563-52034-4

The Ultimate Book of Mind Maps - Tony Buzan
ISBN 978-0-00-721291-0

SPEED READING
Buzan Bites: Speed Reading - Tony Buzan
ISBN 978-0-563-52035-1

REVISION
The Buzan Study Skills Handbook - Tony Buzan
ISBN 978-1-4066-1207-3

LANGUAGES
Collins Language Revolution - Tony Buzan
French - ISBN 978-0-00-725594-8
Spanish - ISBN 978-0-00-725535-1
Italian - ISBN 978-0-00-725511-5

Web Sites

COURSES AND LEARNING TO LEARN

Additional Training
www.learning-tech.co.uk

Speed Reading
www.speedyreader.co.uk

Accelerated Learning
www.learnfast.co.uk

Schools Training
www.inspire-ed.com

SOFTWARE

www.learning-tech.co.uk

MIND SPORTS

www.worldmemorychampionships.com

www.worldmemorysportscouncil.com

www.worldcreativitycouncil.com

The World
Mind Mapping
Council

www.worldmindmappingcouncil.com

www.worldspeedreadingcouncil.com

The World
Speed
Reading
Council

World
I Q
Council

www.worldiqcouncil.com

www.msoworld.com

———————————

Training Services

The authors are available to run seminars in the following techniques…

Mind Mapping
Memory
Speed Reading
Creativity
Time Management
Accelerated Learning
Neuro-Linguistic Programming
Public Open Courses

For further information call:

Phil Chambers on 0845 451 0 451

phil@learning-tech.co.uk or visit www.learning-tech.co.uk

Also by the Authors

A Mind to do Business
ISBN 10: 1-904906-00-1
ISBN 13: 978-1-904906-00-1

The face of business is changing so rapidly that life-long learning has become essential. Our new portfolio careers bring the additional stress of having to continually update our skill-sets to keep our future employment prospects high. The necessity of juggling a full-time job and training requirements with family and home life can push some of us to breaking point.

This book gives you the necessary tools to take control of the information that bombards you on a daily basis; to manage your time; to remember, think and learn more effectively.

Presented in a highly visual and yet structured format with numerous business examples, it allows the reader to quickly grasp and begin to apply the techniques.

101 Top Tips for Better Mind Maps
ISBN 10: 1-904906-02-8
ISBN 13: 978-1-904906-02-5

This book is a distillation of the knowledge and skills that I have gained in over fifteen years of Mind Mapping, ten of which were as an instructor teaching the technique. During this time I have had the privilege of working with and competing against some of the best Mind Mappers in the World. Gradually my style has developed to include some of the best ideas of a range of highly skilled individuals. This culminated in my Gold medal at the 2000 World Championships and winning again in 2004.

My hope is that this book will help you to improve the quality and effectiveness of your own Mind Maps much more rapidly than I managed to through my experiences. Many of the insights that I give are not found in any other book on the subject, making this a unique resource.

Tony Buzan

Buzan Training Ltd

Buzan Training Ltd
24 The Grove
Harleyford Manor Estate
Henley Road
Marlow

Phone: 01628 482 765
Fax: 01628 488 095
E-mail: contactbuzan@buzanworld.com

Visit: www.buzanworld.com

Unleash Genius.

INNOVATIVE LEARNING AND THINKING

Tony Buzan has achieved the status of 'guru', an accolade accorded to very few. He has worked with: corporate entities and businesses all over the world; academics; Olympic athletes; children of all ages; governments; and high profile individuals, in teaching them how to maximise the use of their brain power. Whether he is working one-to-one or delivering a keynote speech to an audience of thousands, his ability to inspire, motivate and empower is awesome.

A prolific author, he has written more than 90 books, with sales in over 150 countries; his books have been translated into at least 33 languages.

Details of most of his publications can be found at

www.buzanbooks.com

Tony's techniques are taught via a global network of Buzan Licensed Instructors in Europe, Asia, the Americas and Australasia.

Discover how to get the most out of Mind Maps PLUS uncover the power of the innovative new Mind Mapping software iMindMap - a brilliant method of presenting big ideas and strategies to any audience.

Develop your own amazing talents - and use the knowledge you acquire to develop the talents of family, friends and colleagues

There are no limits!

VISIT WWW.BUZANWORLD.COM

The UK Schools Memory Championships

The UK Schools Memory Championships has been created to help pupils discover the mind sport of memory and to develop their mental skills to help their studies.

With success in exams dependent on having a good memory, there is no better reason for schools to promote memory clubs and memory competitions for their students. Not many people realise that Memory is a long established Mind Sport and attracts competitors of all ages and from all continents.

Since it was founded in 1991, The World Memory Championships has created a "gold standard" for memory based on ten different memory disciplines. A simplified version of these has now been created specially for schools memory competitions, backed up with a training programme to help teachers to train memory techniques.

This is achieved through an initial training session for a group of up to 30 students and staff introducing the five memory sport disciplines detailed below and a range of mnemonic techniques.

The competition itself is staged in each school lasting approximately half a day. Each school will receive a slightly different set of questions papers to avoid cheating. At the end of the competition each student will receive a ranking and the UK Champion will be announced.

The five memory disciplines are chosen to closely correspond to those in the World Memory Championships:

Random numbers,
Random words,
Fictional events & historic/future dates,
Binary digits,
Memorisation of a shuffled deck of cards (against the clock).

www.schoolsmemorychampionships.com

"Hi, my name is Cando and I want to tell you how those amazing guys at inspire turned my life around.

Man, let me tell you this; before I met those dudes I had a first class ticket to nowhere. I found learning dull and boring. I developed bad habits, poor communication skills and the wrong attitude. My self-esteem was so low that I didn't even believe I had a future, let alone any control over it! I wasn't alone either. Many of my friends felt exactly the same way too.

I'll never forget the day those inspire geezers turned up at our school. I have to admit that I wasn't particularly up for it, in fact I very much doubted that anyone could inspire me at that point in my life. As the session progressed they proved to me that with the right techniques I could develop and improve all of my learning skills. Amazingly, and as corny as it sounds, I did actually start to become inspired by them! I no longer felt like a loser because now I was genuinely engaged and enjoying the whole learning process. Their presentations were not only mesmerising, they were also interactive, practical, creative and most of all great fun! You could tell straight away that these dudes were experts in their field who just loved to inspire others.

I was soon finding that the very same things I struggled with before, and had practically given up on, like maths, science, humanities and languages, were now just a walk in the park for me. I kept having to check myself out to see where those inspire guys had hidden the kryptonite. For with my new enhanced concentration skills, improved memory techniques, reading, writing, and listening skills, along with my superior verbal communication powers, I sure did feel like Superman! Just think, if those crazy dudes at inspire can make someone like me feel like a super hero, imagine what they could do for you! Actually don't just imagine, give them a call and find out for yourself."

Written by Cando Anything (formerly known as Cantdo Anything).

INSPIRE that's what we do best.

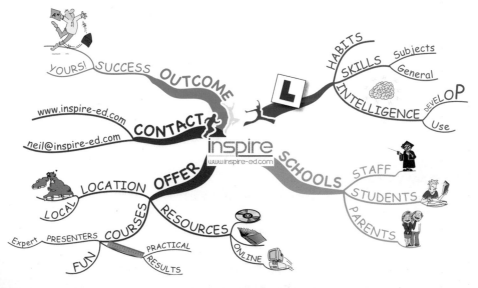